★Take a Break★

Self-Meditate

MEDITATIONS TO SOOTHE YOUR SOUL
& LIFT YOUR SPIRIT

★Take a Break★ *Self-Meditate*

CAROL RICHARDS

Balboa Press books may be ordered through booksellers or by contacting:

Balboa Press
A Division of Hay House
1663 Liberty Drive
Bloomington, IN 47403
www.balboapress.com
1-(877) 407-4847

ISBN: 978-1-4525-6331-2 (e)
ISBN: 978-1-4525-6330-5 (sc)
ISBN: 978-1-4525-6332-9 (hc)

Library of Congress Control Number: 2012921507

Printed in the United States of America

Balboa Press rev. date: 1/2/2013

DEDICATION

This book of meditations is dedicated to my husband, Michael Martineau Richards. His support and loving kindness simultaneously lift me up and keep me grounded. And to my friend and yoga teacher, Maria Glover, for shining her light and brightening my path.

CONTENTS

INTRODUCTION

The writings in this book are from my experiences as I continue to learn to let go and to lovingly accept myself and others. It is important to train our minds to release a need to control the outcome...to go with the flow...to provide space for our minds to interact with life...and to allow our creativity to respond to the variety of situations we encounter. I now understand that trusting life is essential to enjoying life.

As I progress along my path, encountering both pain and peace, I continually remind myself to choose happiness. This becomes a challenge when our daily lives appear to spin out of control; and we place more obligations and duties on ourselves. Often, people look to drugs or alcohol to take away the anxiety and stress.

When you feel stretched to your limit, instead of *self-medicating*, why not try something different? **Take A Break and Self-Meditate.** Open to any page in this book. Take a few minutes to go within and listen to your Higher Self. Learn to be your own healing source. Allow yourself to soothe your soul and lift your spirit. Wonders will unfold as you connect with your true self.

BE PRESENT

APPRECIATE THE GIFTS

Be present to each phase of your life; this will enable you to appreciate all the gifts as they are offered. If you are married, recognize that it is a wonderful stage of life. And, it is different than being single. When you are married, it's a blessing to enjoy life with your partner. There are many challenges in learning to share the same living space, day in and day out; but, there are also many rewards. The beauty and comfort of waking up in the arms of someone, who loves you unconditionally, is a joy that soothes your soul and lifts your spirit. Learning how to balance both of your needs with honesty, respect and love is a lesson in embracing the beauty of relationships. Patience, kindness, fidelity and trust are all different streets in the same neighborhood - a perfect place to call home. It is a destination, not easily arrived at, but much appreciated. Remember, we learn about ourselves, and how to be our best, when we give ourselves completely and lovingly to a committed relationship.

BE IN THE MOMENT

Meditation provides an opportunity to shut out distractions; focus on the present; and tune into your inner voice. Allow it to help train your mind to be in the moment. Practice breathing and being fully aware of your body. Feel the sensation of each movement, the pull of your muscles, the sensation of the fabric stretching across your skin. Acquaint yourself with the tension in your neck, the weight of your legs as you lift them. Breathe into those parts of your body that need release. Allow your body to loosen up, relax, and return to its natural state. We are trained "doers." But we are so much more than what we do. We are human *beings* and our natural highs come from "being" in the moment and enjoying the wonder of life's experiences. Use meditation to help you be present to all that you can be.

EMBRACE IMPERMANENCE

The process of life is change and impermanence. Babies grow to children, children to adults, adults to seniors, and seniors pass away. This impermanence of life actually enhances its value. Accepting the impermanence enables us to better value each stage of our lives - as we know it will not last. But, still, we often take our lives for granted. When someone is ill and told they have a finite amount of time left, they usually look at life differently and start to treasure each moment. The truth is we all have a finite amount of time to live and none of us know the length of that time. Let us embrace the impermanence, open ourselves up to a deeper sense of gratitude, and awaken to the gift of life.

FOLLOW YOUR HEART; CHOOSE JOY

Daily life may overwhelm you with choices. But, once again, staying present will allow you to dial into your own guidance and make the best choice you can at that moment. Many of our decisions are confusing because we come to them from a place of fear. Instead, accept that we are all on an amazing adventure. There are so many paths from which to choose; and you cannot go wrong when you follow your heart. Relax into each day's blessings and continually *choose* joy in order to receive the gifts of grace that await you.

FULLY ENGAGE

Whenever there is an opportunity to share words of wisdom, encourage people to fully engage in each stage of their journey. Help others know that their present circumstances will shift as life is constantly changing and evolving. We are alive to create, grow, learn and move through the phases of our lives. True happiness materializes when you focus on each page of your story *as it is being written.* By appreciating every chapter of your life, you open yourself up to living in a state of joy. And joy begets more joy. There are unending avenues to pursue with a variety of treasures to discover. Be present; and open your heart to enjoy it all.

IN JOY THE SHOW

Avoid fretting about yesterday or worrying about tomorrow. Instead, practice IN JOYING the moment. It is difficult to be IN JOY if you are overwhelmed or distracted by the need to juggle too many things at once. These distractions reduce your awareness, create confusion and make it hard to hear the healing guidance of your intuition. When you live this way, you end up missing the happenings of your own life. Instead, make the most of the opportunities to unwrap the gifts contained in each day. So, take a deep breath, sit back, relax and IN JOY the show.

IT IS WHAT IT IS

It is what it is. These words are heard frequently as it has become a common phrase in our culture. They signify an important part of our path to fully accept the present. This does not mean you are a passive participant in your own life. On the contrary, these words remind us to balance acceptance with effort. Continually encourage your Spirit to strive to be all that you can be and then sweetly surrender to life on its terms. Release fear and cherish what is.

THE TIME OF YOUR LIFE

Oftentimes, we don't appreciate what we have at that moment. Instead, we wish we were somewhere else further down the road in our journey. For example, if you are single, you may spend an inordinate amount of time dwelling on when your *soul mate* will appear. Instead, enjoy this phase to learn about yourself and what you truly desire and deserve. While longing for a perfect partner is normal and healthy, putting our lives on hold until then is not. We would benefit by recognizing that being single offers so many choices and the freedom to explore: opportunities to grow more comfortable in your own skin; to learn to be true to yourself; to find your voice; to safely separate from your parents; and to learn to be your own best friend. Make the most of this single stage of your life for it is the time of your life.

TO-BE LIST

Does your life ever feel like a never ending to-do list? Such lists draw us to focus on keeping track of chores, errands, goals and projects that need attention. And, while it is momentarily satisfying to cross off the next task, that feeling is fleeting. Several other items seem to immediately replace the one accomplishment. Instead of making a list and checking it twice, and twice again, why not consider creating a to-be list. It is not necessary to compose this list on paper. Rather, concentrate on what you want your life to be. Imagine being happy, peaceful, joyful, healthy and prosperous. Initiate these intentions in your mind and then feel the pleasant emotions connected with them. The more you focus on being, the easier the doing becomes, and a joyful life is realized.

WINNERS MUST BE PRESENT

As you have heard at raffle drawings, WINNERS MUST BE PRESENT. Meditation helps us to stay present. By concentrating on our breath, we focus on the ins and outs of each inhale and exhale. By training our minds to be quiet and enjoy each breath, each moment, each pose, we are better able to appreciate the ins and outs of our lives. All the power of each moment is in the PRESENT. We cannot change the past or control the future, but we can be present to the NOW. How often do we miss what is actually happening to us and around us because we are focused on something someone said yesterday or what we need to do tomorrow? Practice being present to your own life...it is a gift. Enjoy the power it wields to make you a winner.

BREATHE INTO BALANCE

BREATHE IN; BREATHE OUT

The word, Spirit, is from the Latin "spiritus," which means breath. Our spirit is the gift of life, the provider of all things. Without our breath, our bodies cannot function and Spirit passes from our physical form. As we breathe, we infuse life into every cell. Breathe in; breathe out. That is what meditation and yoga is all about. The word, yoga, is Sanskrit for "union." As we breathe into each pose, we are uniting our mind, body and spirit. We seek balance with each inhale; we seek release with each exhale. Breathe in; breathe out. Allow love, light, laughter, healthfulness, harmony and joy to flow. Let the steady rhythm of our spirit calm us; recharge our energy; and rekindle our passions.

EQUILIBRIUM

Do you ever feel like you are on a never ending seesaw, striving to find balance in your life, as you cope with the ups and downs and ins and outs of the human experience? Life is about dualities and seemingly conflicting ideas. It is simultaneously simple and complex; dark and light; up and down. A fulfilled spirit strives for balance, to sustain peace and happiness, while recognizing that life is full of paradoxes. We need to learn to give and receive; work and play; laugh and cry; soar and fall in order to experience the full range of life's landscape. Our ability to realign, and continually correct, assures we are never pulled completely off course. So, today, in your quest for equilibrium, appreciate how you teeter and totter; then redirect and breathe into balance.

FACE YOUR FEARS

Face your fears. Look them straight in the eye; confront the concerns and learn what makes them linger. Let go of the need to engage them in a struggle as fighting only makes them stronger. In order to loosen their grip, slowly pry away the fingers of fear clutching your heart. Remember you have grown stronger with your spiritual practice. You no longer need to be scared of these ghosts of despair. They may be a pattern to release; a wrong to forgive or a misdeed to correct. Recognize that the demons lurking behind the closet door are of our own making. When we give more power to these demons, they grow big and strong and loom ever larger. We must acknowledge that the past is over. We begin anew with each breath. We have nothing to fear but what we create with our minds.

INSPIRE YOURSELF

Meditation is a wonderful way to gain inspiration for our daily lives. The word, "inspire," means to breathe in spirit. All our poses incorporate our breath. It is an integral part of our practice and our lives. We cannot live without our breath; we cannot live without spirit. When a soul departs from a body, all you see is the physical shell of the person. The spirit, the breath, has left. Our breath connects us to our Divine Source, which brings us peace, nourishment, healing, balance and joy. During your practice today, remember to breathe deeply and allow your body to relax completely. Breathe in; breathe out; create a deeper connection to your source. Go higher and inspire yourself.

LET GO OF EXPECTATIONS

Expectations versus intentions – the ability to discern the subtle difference between the two is a wonderful skill. We must intend positive results, in order to manifest our heart's desires; but, we also need to let go of expectations. Firm expectations can actually block our greatest good from arriving. Close your eyes and imagine fully opening your heart to receive God's blessings. As we empty ourselves of expectations, we provide space for the proverbial *cup to runneth over.* Strive for a neutral mindset and stay positive in your intentions. Practice this all while being open and trusting as to what the future will bring. This delicate balancing act may appear to be a dichotomy but it is an important key to our heightened happiness. Our Divine Source is limitless; let us not be the ones to place limiting expectations on God's graces.

POSITIVE OUTLOOK

We all recognize that a positive attitude has far reaching benefits. It colors everything and enhances our *experiences* in a genuine way. Maintaining that positive outlook can be a challenge; but it is always a choice. We all encounter daily difficulties. What we do, when we come face to face with our frustrations, makes the difference between a joyful or sour disposition. It is important to first acknowledge that we have a choice as to how we react. Then, select the next best step to take; and move forward on your path. In order to assist in adjusting your outlook, remember your meditation tools to help your mind switch gears. Take a moment to breathe; walk about; change your focus; or talk to a friend. Even a small adjustment can mentally move you from frustration to acceptance. Choose wisely; choose joy.

SWEET SPOT

Let us consider what we would like to manifest in our lives. Take a few minutes to consciously plant your seeds of intention. We can then lovingly cultivate them with our practice. As we reach and stretch our minds and bodies past our comfort zone, remember to seek that sweet spot – that place of effort and surrender. Extend to the edge, as we further challenge ourselves, while still maintaining a focused ease and strength. Remain mindful to avoid over reaching or struggling to hold a painful position. Seek equilibrium with effort, but not force. This is the sweet surrender that allows us to grow and evolve and trust that we are moving in the right direction. Let us strive forth with balance and watch as our intentions blossom and grow.

TRUE PERFECTION

The pursuit of perfection poisons a soul and robs the spirit of joy. Struggling to do what we believe we "*should*" is not a path to peace. We are bombarded with advice on how to manifest our best lives – we *should* save for retirement; we *should* refinance our homes; we *should* floss our teeth; we *should* take time to exercise and meditate; we *should* stay in touch with friends and family; and on and on the list grows. These are all important and beneficial reminders. But, when they start to create stress, they no longer serve our well being. We are wired to want to be the best that we can be. But, when life is crowded out with "*shoulds,*" bliss is missed. Our soul resents this pressure and finds a way to shout: **Don't *should* on me.** So, once again, let us seek balance in our lives. Release the need to be perfect and do the best we can with joyful hearts. We are here to love and be loved and that is true perfection.

LET GO AND FOLLOW THE FLOW

ART OF LETTING GO

Sometimes, we realize our time with someone has drawn to a close; and we are "meant" to move on. But, letting go is often a struggle, even when you know it is the right thing to do for the good of all involved. It may feel like you have to be dragged, kicking and screaming, into your own future. Remember, the art of letting go is a matter of practice; and it is important to develop this skill. There are always plenty of opportunities to learn to let go as daily life experience is the master teacher. Let go; and life will amaze you with irony. Because, when you let go of what you have "struggled" to attain, it comes flowing right to you. *OR NOT.* And, if not, then it was not necessary to be present in your life; and, by letting go, you have freed yourself to attract and receive something better.

DANCE WITH LIFE

Learn to dance with life. Lean into the experience and become its partner. Do not fight the flow; but, rather, sweetly surrender. Move the matter along by becoming part of it. Let go of the struggle; release to the rhythm of life. Follow your instincts and be keenly aware of your circumstances. Observe and respond appropriately with just the right amount of energy for that particular situation. Roll with the punches. Dance with the dream. Manifest your desires. Claim power over your own life. Direct with your desires and lead yourself forward to your promised land.

EASY, PEASY, LEMON SQUEEZY

Easy, Peasy, Lemon Squeezy...let's borrow a line from this children's rhyme and have fun with our practice today. Let's play; feel free, fun and fluid as we smile and sway to the twists and turns of our bodies. Be light and breezy... *Easy, Peasy, Lemon Squeezy.* Let go of the stress; let go of our mind's chatter, and follow the flow. Let life be. Relish in the rhythm of your movements. Smile on the inside; send your body a big hug; laugh with your heart and enjoy the moment. *Easy, Peasy, Lemon Squeezy.*

FAITH VS. STUBBORNNESS

Faith is a quiet trust in God's will; while stubbornness is an obstinate insistence on our will. How often do we get ingrained in our positions and call that faith? When, in reality, it is just stretched-out stubbornness. We are trained to set forth our desires with determination and commitment. But, tenaciously holding on, to what we want to manifest, is not the same intent. Learn to let your wishes be known but balance them with acceptance. Fully trust that you will receive "this or something better." Only when we faithfully open ourselves up to receive the answers to our prayers, can we then be granted our deserved desires. Once again, remember to release and surrender to the Divine plan. Let go of attempts to control the outcome of your longings. Relax into the sweet, safe embrace of the Universe with the confidence that your needs will always be well provided. Know that the best is yet to come.

FOLLOW THE FLOW

Follow the flow...the flow of our breath...the flow of our bodies...the flow of life's course. When we truly believe that our Divine Source is watching out for us, then we can easily let go and follow the flow. Except, too often, we want to be in control of the ride. We want to dictate how our journey evolves. But, true happiness lies in letting our Divine Source direct the flow of traffic. Our role is to trust and enjoy what is placed on our path. Embrace and live through each challenge, each pleasure and each crisis. Treat them all as opportunities for appreciating the gift of life and our ability to think, feel, evolve and mature. Relax and reside in the knowledge that God is leading us towards our greater good, all of the time.

GRACE AND GRATITUDE

Grace and gratitude go hand in hand with an ease of being. When we embrace and appreciate what is, we are better able to experience joy and peace. Practice an attitude of gratitude; accept what is; and enable yourself to celebrate all aspects of your journey. Allow meditation to guide you to a deeper sense of contentment by being grateful for what you have rather than longing for what you don't. Relish in the successes, as well as the challenges, you encounter. You will be positively transformed as you learn to release resistance and go with the flow of your life.

LET GO OF ATTACHMENTS

An important spiritual principle is to train the mind to let go of attachments to predetermined outcomes. Our culture trains us to be doers with set goals to achieve. We become obsessed and stressed when we strive to ensure our goals happen *as we think they are supposed to happen.* When our thoughts get locked in, we choke off the life force by blocking its flow and limiting the space for ideas to grow. Practice the dance of life; listen to the beat of your drum; play it as you hear it; intend for the best; and follow the flow. You'll be surprised where it takes you and what gifts await you.

RECOGNIZE AND RELEASE

Letting go...this is often easier said than done... even of the things that no longer serve our well being. Patterns of negative behaviors, relationships or thoughts can be difficult to recognize and release. They can feel like "old friends" with whom we have grown accustomed to sharing our life. Practice letting go of such negativity. Train yourself to connect with your own true nature of love and light. Recognize those things that cause needless suffering. Every time we show up to meditate, we cultivate a deeper sense of inner peace. This calmness strengthens and centers us as we progress towards positive change. Once we recognize and release what is no longer constructive or healthy, we make room for choices that foster growth and happiness. Remember your spiritual practice is a pathway to peace and a gateway to your heart light. Let go and follow the flow.

SWEETLY SURRENDER

By sweetly surrendering to Divine will, the ties that bind you are loosened. Energy is allowed to flow through you and to you. The channels are then flooded with all the blessings that are your Divine right. This is my interpretation of the meaning of free will: choosing to allow God to grant your heart's desires by opening yourself up to receive; while, simultaneously, surrendering to that higher power and trusting that all is for your greatest good. Remember, the Universe beckons us to recognize and revel in the glory of our individual adventures. As each day dawns, let us purposely and passionately choose to live our best lives.

TRUST THE CURRENT

Learning how to truly go with flow is an important skill for maneuvering the currents of life. We all know how it feels to be paddling against the current; because, no matter how hard we paddle, we don't get where we want to go. It is important to put our boat in the water, point it in the desired direction, and then allow the tide to take us there. You would not put your boat in the water if you didn't think the river would take you to a desired destination. So, we need to trust the current. We further enhance this ride by discerning when to paddle fast and hard; when to take the oars out of the water and float like a leaf in a stream; and when to paddle evenly and smoothly. Remember, we do not need to struggle if we are pointed in the right direction. We just need to go with the flow.

PASS THE PEACE

CHOOSE PEACE

Remember, our resistance to evolving events can turn our journey into a painful climb. Focus your mind around "embracing" the perceived negative circumstances. When one appreciates that there are gifts to unwrap, wherever we find ourselves, we have then discovered the gateway to happiness. Be grateful for all the supposed "setbacks" because they are your best teachers. The maturity and wisdom, gleaned from all of life's lessons, will instill the insight that the joy is in the journey. Cultivate gratitude for the experience; and choose peace over pain.

MOVE ON TOWARDS PEACE

Do you ever feel like you are moving and grooving, happily going with the flow, and pretty proud of yourself for handling all the ups and downs of life in a positive manner? Then, seemingly out of the blue, another frustrating circumstance crosses your path and you get totally bothered. Is it the endless list of demands on your time; the relentless whining of a coworker; or a fear that your finances will continue to be drained with unforeseen expenditures? We all experience these types of irritations. But, once again, we have a choice. We can allow them to continue to annoy us, or we can choose to learn from these triggering events. Seek to know what is driving the resentment and determine your next best step. Does a fear need to be released; do you need to just chuckle at human foibles; or does an action step need to be taken? Choose well and move on towards peace.

PASS THE PEACE

We all encounter relationship challenges. They can include dealing with a difficult coworker, healing hurt feelings, reassuring a loved one, or accepting ourselves at a deeper level. We want to do the right thing to bring peace and harmony to the situation. But, what is the right thing? Our inner guidance knows the path to peace and it usually involves acknowledging our own frustrations, anger and pain. And, then releasing those feelings; choosing to rise higher; and reaching out with love. Words are not always necessary. Loving feelings sent from one spirit to another also soothe and comfort. When you find yourself puzzled as to how to attain peace, breathe; acknowledge your own feelings; respectfully release them; and send healing love and light to the circumstances. You will relax and feel more peaceful. And, while we cannot control how others receive this love, please know, on some level, they will feel the energy shift and the situation will soften. Pass the Peace.

PATH OF PEACE

We often do not take notice of how blessed we are until we are thrown off balance. We then usually set our sights on regaining our equilibrium. But, once we have achieved that, we may deceivingly think: *OK, now I am going to avoid suffering. I know how to attract happiness and let go of negative circumstances. I'm going to control my life and stay centered.* But, in truth, we cannot know what tomorrow will bring or what circumstances will provide a chance for peace or pain. To help ease the anxiety, it is comforting to remember that all we have is this day. Today is the day to practice being present to your life; today is the day to be kind; today is the day to make your best choices. Life is not a stagnant stalemate; it is alive and fluid. Seek balance with each moment, as it unfolds, and you will find yourself firmly planted on the path of peace.

PEACEFUL WARRIOR

As we move through life, let us remember to be alert and aware in a calm and tranquil manner. Mimic the practice of the peaceful warrior. He or she does not promote violence nor maliciously attack others. Yet, the peaceful warrior is ever present to surrounding danger and ever ready to skillfully defend against aggression. A neutral balance is struck between harmony and the necessity to thwart an assault. Practice averting hostile attempts to engage in battle whenever possible. But, be unafraid to stand up for what is right and safeguard your space.

PERSONAL PEACE

To continue on a path of opening our heart to self-love, let us remember to not be distracted by an unbalanced need for external approval. We must show ourselves unwavering love and respect. We must learn to appreciate ourselves regardless of what others think. Look to be your own anchor in the wind. If you tie your happiness to the shifting currents of other's perceptions and goals, you will be blown off course, unable to chart your own happiness. Listen to what the critics say; and, if you determine changes are needed, make them. But, don't allow yourself to be dragged down into despair and self-hatred. Treat yourself as you treat others. Be kind and gentle. Recall what Jesus said: Love thy neighbor as thyself. Self-love is always the way. This is the path to personal peace.

PERSONAL POWER

When we become frustrated and angry at others, it is easy to blame our feelings on their actions. But, that is never the true cause. We are responsible for our own feelings and how we react to circumstances. Let go of this victim mentality and claim your own personal power. Allow others to be themselves but remain unafraid that they will unduly influence you. Recognize that they cannot cause you pain without your permission. Remember, you are the master of your emotions. People's actions may annoy you as they pursue their personal agendas. So, train your mind in mental martial arts. Step aside from these attacks on your ego. Don't directly resist. Move into the circumstance and manage it. This is the best way to control the situation. This choice affords you the freedom of deciding how you want to react and what the next best step is for personal peace and joy.

REFLECTIONS OF THE SEASONS

BEAUTIFUL BEGINNING TO THE YEAR

When one year ends and another begins, what do you remember most? What challenges have you faced? What opportunities were presented to you? What lessons have you learned? What changes have you made to improve your life and the lives of those around you? The beginning of the year is always a great time to reflect on the happenings of the past 12 months. It is also an important time to set your intentions for the year ahead. What would you like to accomplish? What do you want your life to look like in the New Year? What words would you choose to describe the upcoming year? Listen to your inner voice and visualize all you want the year to bring to you.

CIRCLE OF LIFE

Our outer world is a reflection of the transformations we experience in our inner world. Take some time and go outside to observe the circle of life's surroundings. Nature is a generous guide as it showcases the seasons. It teaches us to trust that life is following a Divine plan. Seasonal changes are an inherent part of human nature too. Except, people tend to embrace change only when it is perceived to be beneficial. We tend to resist what we don't want. Trees do not lament the falling of their leaves; birds do not refuse to fly south for the winter; bears do not go kicking and screaming into hibernation. Plants, birds and animals trust their instinctive nature. They are masters of embracing change and following the flow of what is happening now. Learn from their example. Build that inner trust. Breathe; let go and know your current cycle is a perfect part of the circle of life.

LEAP DAY

Leap day occurs once every four years. It is a calculated coordination to more closely align our calendar with the earth's revolutions around the sun. Wouldn't it be nice if there was a scheduled correction for each of us when we get out of balance? A marvelous method designed to sync us with our surroundings and reconnect us to our higher selves. Self-meditation is a tried and true approach to accomplish this. When you feel out of sorts, off-balance or out-of-sync with yourself, remember to take a few moments to relax and reconnect. Quiet your mind; breathe and hold the intention to bring peace to your situation. You will be amazed at the power of a meditation moment to bring you back to who you truly are.

SPIRITUAL SPROUTING

The seasons change, as we progress through the calendar year, and offer clear signs of the ongoing metamorphosis on planet Earth. Oftentimes, the proof of transformation, along our personal paths, is not as easily recognizable. But, when we look back to observe the milestones of our life, we can see the maturation process unfolding. And, just as seedlings pushing through the Earth herald the start of Spring, our propelling forward through difficulties symbolizes our spiritual sprouting. We deepen our roots and strengthen our foundation as we spiritually grow. This lays the groundwork for our continued ability to reach higher and stand stronger. Let us remember to lovingly tend our spiritual seedlings with kindness and grace so that we may fully bloom as God intended.

SUMMER SOLSTICE

Summer Solstice is the day when the earth is most inclined towards the Sun, resulting in the year's longest period of daylight. For centuries, people have celebrated the Summer Solstice with festivals and religious ceremonies. They reveled in the rhythm of the seasons - the culmination of a cold winter; the planting of seeds in Spring; the warmth of Summer; and the knowledge that Autumn would herald the completion of the cycle. But, for this day, they rejoiced and honored the light that shines upon us and within us. As the Sun's bright light enables the Earth to thrive, so does our Eternal Light enable our Spirits to flourish. Let us lean into the light of God's love; radiate our inner glow; and allow our own lives to blaze brightly and illuminate the way.

THANKSGIVING

Thanksgiving is a perfect time to turn our attention to the bounty of blessings in our lives. So often, we lose track of all the good we have been given. It seems easier to look at what we don't have and forget that we have so much. An attitude of gratitude is the quickest way to reconnect with our Divine Source and open the door to continued abundance. Let's make every day a day of thanksgiving. Let us remember things great and small that enhance our experience. Take note of 10 things for which you are grateful. While it is essential to appreciate good health; family and friends; our homes and jobs, include items that you may not normally consider . . . an American's freedom to choose; a warm bed and clean sheets; the wide variety of food on your table; the ability to use your limbs; the convenience of a garage door opener; or your pet's unconditional love. We are blessed beyond belief and need only to celebrate this cornucopia of abundance to know true joy.

UNWRAP THE GREATEST GIFT

Let's take a moment to send our spirits love and appreciation for meditating today. It can be challenging to take time for oneself during the busy holiday season. Make an opportunity to relax, to breathe and to reflect on the reason for the season. This is a wonderful gift to lavish on ourselves. AND it is a gift that keeps on giving. We all have many distractions and excuses that attempt to pull us away from a few minutes of meditation. But, by honoring our commitment to our bodies and spirits, we replenish our energy and our enthusiasm. This inner smile will help carry us through the holidays by opening up space for more joy. So, as you relax into your body, remember the true meaning of the holidays is to share love. That is the greatest gift of all.

WINTER SOLSTICE

On December 21, the day of Winter Solstice, we experience the longest night of the year. As we plunge into the depths of darkness, it is a natural time for introspection. Consider the challenges experienced during the past year. Welcome an opportunity to learn from them and carry this knowledge forward to better yourself. Allow this "dark night of the soul" to transform you. Accept the darkness; embrace your shadows. Then, celebrate and rejoice at your inner awareness that the light will once again return. Prepare the way for this illumination and feed your dreams with faith. Practice hope for it is the springboard by which we propel ourselves onward and upward. So, amidst the hustle and bustle of your holiday preparations, please take some time to acknowledge the darkness and prepare your spirit for the rebirth of the light in each of us.

YEAR END'S BRIGHT LIGHT

The day after Winter Solstice, when the amount of daily darkness reached its deepest depth, the light again begins to grow brighter and longer with each new day. It is a poignant reminder that, as soon as we reached the bottom of this darkness, we immediately began the cyclical climb back to the light. This symbol of eternal life is of great importance for the human race and has been marked by celebrations for thousands of years. Christmas signifies the bright light being reborn into our world, as do the Celtic celebration of Solstice and the Hebrew festival of Hanukah. Spirit's innate longing for the light is crystallized by the celebration of the Christ Child's birth and his promise that he is the light and the way. Let us follow his great example and shine our lights brightly throughout the holidays and into the New Year. Peace on earth and goodwill to all.

SHINE YOUR LIGHT

FLY HIGH

According to Disney's baby elephant, Dumbo: "The very things that held you down are going to carry you up." You may recall the challenges that little Dumbo faced, when he was separated from his mom, and had to deal with being teased, taunted and treated as an outsider. But, even with the difficulties he encountered, he remained a loving, positive creature. He allowed himself time to feel sad and lonely, but he did not stay there. He believed in life and all that it had to offer. He went out and literally lifted himself up, using the very part of him which had been ridiculed by others. His large ears became his wings and his spirit soared. Let us each discover our own wings and learn to fly high by turning difficulties into opportunities. Be all that you can be. Shine your light, through the darkness, for all to see.

HEART LIGHT

Compassion and courage – these are two traits that comprise the essence of our heart light. Compassion is merciful tenderness which opens our hearts to consider other people's perspectives. We can then treat them with respect regardless of our thoughts about their actions. Courage is the ability to move forward in spite of our fears and self-imposed limitations. When we seek to do the right thing, from our heart, even if it's not what our ego wants, we come from a place of true courage. Let us continue to marry these two traits and create a union which allows us to shine and share our heart's true light.

ILLUMINATE YOUR PATH

The only way to really control your life is to be responsible for your own choices and your own reactions. Do not allow fear, anger and rage to blind you to reality. These emotions are usually, somehow, directed at ourselves. If we feel we are undeserving, unloved or not good enough, we succumb to suffering. Stop this senseless self-punishment and self-ridicule. We all have a shadow side. Do not condemn this part of your psyche. Instead, acknowledge its presence and gently loosen its grip. Breathe acceptance into its embrace and allow your shadow to show you the way. Shine your light brightly into the darkness. Illuminate the path before you and move forward to peace.

LOVING KINDNESS

Yes; it is important to learn to be loving and kind; but, it is also important to be clear about your motives. Otherwise, acts of loving kindness can be manipulative and controlling. Setting healthy boundaries is an important step in clarifying these intentions. True loving kindness is a selfless act performed without the expectation of getting anything in return. It comes from compassion and connection, not from a need for approval and companionship. You give merely because you want to share and that feels good. Set an intention to be of service to others and recognize that practicing loving kindness is its own reward. This opens you up to successful sharing. An inner knowing will blossom as you benefit from the blessings that sprout from the seeds of loving kindness you have sown.

NAMASTE

"*Namaste*" is the Sanskrit word used to communicate that: "*The Divine light in me greets the Divine light in you.*" This is a reflection of your inner core, your true self, which is pure light and love...your heart light. Whatever challenges you face today, remember to go inward and reconnect to that spark of divinity. When you look into your mirror, see this reflection of the Divine light within you. Allow it to radiate outward for all to see. Shine your heart light and share love. And, when you look at someone else, remember to see this same spark shining through their eyes. Be the light you want to see and look for that light in all faces and all places. *Namaste.*

PERFECTLY FLAWED

Human beings are flawed. We are perfectly flawed; but flawed nonetheless. One of our most important lessons is to learn to love ourselves and others, completely, and that includes our flaws. This is a crucial cornerstone of spiritual evolution. We must look at our blemishes and recognize they are blessed manifestations of being human. Like a diamond in the rough, we may polish the flaws until they shine; but, they remain part of the package. And, if we are willing to accept and work with these flaws, we can overcome the negativity that arises from them. We can actually build upon this knowledge to be the best that we can be.

PERSONAL FLIGHT

Self-love is the foundation upon which we build a healthy, fulfilling life. Without self-love, we do not take proper care of ourselves on any level. In order to manifest our best lives and see our intentions blossom, we must look at our roots. Are there unresolved issues we still feel guilty about? Is there pain from the past that needs to be healed? is there forgiveness to be granted to ourselves and others? Or, are there choices about diet and exercise that need to be made? Please remember that we must have a solid foundation upon which to build. Clean out leftover debris and clutter from your life and think about ways to fill in any cracks. This is your time to soar and shine; so, please create a solid base upon which you can launch your personal flight.

TRUE LOVE

Attracting true love begins with first learning to love oneself. We can become so focused on "earning" love and giving love, in order to receive love, we forget to honor ourselves. We are often our own worst critics and may feel undeserving of God's grace. And, while it may seem counter intuitive, we need to learn how to receive the gift of unconditional love. This gift begins with loving oneself. Negativity towards oneself actually blocks the attainment of true love. Recognize that you are worthy of being loved, for who you are, not just for what you do. When we open to receive this gift of self-love and acceptance, we can truly love and accept others. And, then this true love can be mirrored back to us.

WORTHY OF LOVE

The key to living a joyful life is to love ourselves and others at our highest potential. And, in order to truly love, it is essential to possess a healthy feeling of self-worth and self-respect. It is important to know *and always remember* that we are all worthy of love - just because we are. We don't have to earn love. We don't have to do things to make others love us or prove that we are worthy. We just need to be. TRUST that unconditional love is a gift from the Creator; our gift to share and enjoy. There are no stipulations placed on pure love and that begins within our own hearts.

TRUST YOUR INNER GUIDANCE

DEFINE YOURSELF

Sensitivity must be tempered with strength or it will weaken you from the inside out. Do not allow other people's views to feed your fears and play on your insecurities. You are not well served whenever you give your power away in this manner. Instead, drama and discontent are drawn into your life. Honor yourself by setting healthy boundaries. Do not allow others to define you. Define yourself. You alone are responsible for how you feel; how you respond; how you choose to live. Self-respect is the foundation for loving yourself and the stepping stone to accepting humanity. Compassion will be the natural byproduct of this environment; and sensible sensitivity can be realized.

INTERNAL COMPASS

Let us use our spiritual intentions as our internal compass, the guiding star by which we steer our lives. Consciously focus on the direction you want your life to take. Choose your intentions wisely and lovingly as they will serve as navigation tools. We may not always follow the directions as we are prone to go adrift. But, be gentle with yourself as you reposition your feet along your chosen way. We must remember to continually correct our course and mindfully redirect ourselves back towards our intentions. Our ego mind is expert at distracting us from our purposeful path as it seeks to lead us astray. Align and realign your internal compass with your own north star; and allow it to lead you back home no matter how far you have strayed.

OUR GUIDING STAR

Let us lovingly and gently set aside our egos so we can tune in to our higher self. Meditation is the ideal companion for mentally stepping away from our "small" mind and attending to our heart's true desires. This access is always available to quietly guide you. But, too often, the noise of daily life drowns out its sound. We must take time for our own voice to be heard and carefully cultivate our soul connection. So, take a deep breath; enter your inner stillness; and listen for that soft, subtle voice gently guiding you home – a place to pursue your passion and from which to make your best choices. Let's take advantage of our guiding star and gladly go where it directs us.

PERSONAL NAVIGATION SYSTEM

Have you ever felt anxious or cautious and not really known why? An answer is always available by going within and asking your higher self: "*Why do I feel this way? What do I need to know?*" Practice turning off the mindless chatter in your head. Clear the static from the line and tune into the guide within. We come equipped with our own personal navigation system so listen as your Spirit speaks. Intuition always steers us in the right direction. We just need to practice the art of listening and become familiar with this voice. Test it out; ask a question; and be receptive to the reply. See how it feels to follow your own personal navigation system. Then, watch what destinations you attain.

POSITIVE PRONOUNCEMENTS

In order to love anyone else, we must first learn to love ourselves. A fun activity, to nurture self-love, is to create your own positive affirmations. And then repeat them to yourself every day. For example: *I admire and respect myself. I enjoy perfect personal and professional partnerships. Love, light and laughter surround me. I experience terrific travel adventures. My path is blessed with peace and prosperity. I trust myself to make the best choice at the time.* Write down the emotions you want to feel in your heart about yourself or what loving acceptance you long to hear. Then, look in the mirror and say at least one loving comment to yourself every day. You will be amazed at the impact this will have on your outlook on life and the positive results that show up in your relationships, particularly the one with yourself.

REMAIN CALM

The path to deepening self-love is not always smooth. Along the way, you will surely encounter pain. This is your heart healing the hurt. Your soul is grieving the letting go and dissolution of habits that no longer serve you. How often do we pray for gifts from God, and then question how they are wrapped and delivered? We wonder how these gifts could lead us to such sorrow, loss and discomfort. This is when we have an opportunity to commit to our self-growth. We must TRUST that all is occurring for our greater good. Be still; sit with the discomfort; and pray for the transmutation of pain into peace. If we can remain calm during the storm, we will surely be shown the way and dive deeper into the sea of self-love.

TRUST YOUR INNER VOICE

As you progress along your path, beware of all the distractions that can move you away from happiness. It is easy to become frustrated and annoyed when we don't feel like we are where we "should" be or want to be. We waste so much of our present lives wishing it away. We long for what we had and dwell on the past and what might have been. Or, we spend countless hours ruminating about what the future will bring. Such focus actually moves you away from a joyful life. It may appear overwhelming to switch gears, and be grateful for what is, while excitedly looking forward to the future. The way through these torturous thoughts is to learn from the past; move forward; and become better, not bitter. Ask yourself: "How much of my life has been lost by not being present to what is happening right now?" Trust your inner voice's response and unlock the message in your heart as it cries out for joy.

ABOUT THE AUTHOR

CAROL CERRONE RICHARDS lives in Las Vegas, Nevada, with her husband and their family of dogs and kitties. She enjoys reading, writing, hiking and traveling, particularly in the mountains and at the beach. Carol also does volunteer work with child welfare advocacy groups. She has been employed in the paralegal profession and had articles appear in legal publications. As a long time student of yoga and spiritual growth, she began writing these meditations for an office yoga group. It is her sincere desire that this book will help guide your soul to a place of peace, and lift your spirit higher, so that you may live your life with a joyful, loving heart.

★ Self-Meditations to Soothe Your Soul

& Lift Your Spirit ★

★ Self-Meditations to Soothe Your Soul

& Lift Your Spirit ★

★ Self-Meditations to Soothe Your Soul

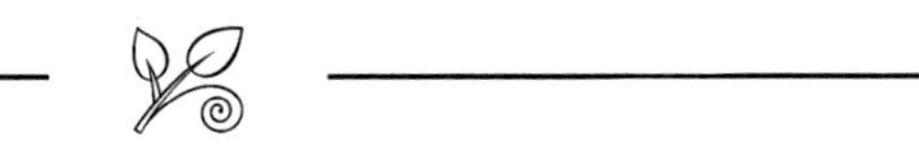

& Lift Your Spirit ★

★ Self-Meditations to Soothe Your Soul

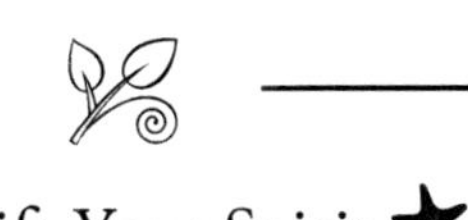

& Lift Your Spirit ★

★ Self-Meditations to Soothe Your Soul

& Lift Your Spirit ★

★ Self-Meditations to Soothe Your Soul

& Lift Your Spirit ★

CPSIA information can be obtained at www.ICGtesting.com
Printed in the USA
BVOW08s1524130813

328436BV00001B/2/P